THE
90DAY
CREDIT
CHALLENGE

90DAY CREDIT CHALLENGE

PLAYING THE GAME
OF CREDIT SCORING
KNOW THE RULES
TO WIN!

Jeanne Kelly

EPIGRAPH BOOKS

RHINEBECK, NY

The 90-Day Credit Challenge: Playing the Game of Credit Scoring —
Know the Rules to Win! Copyright © 2011 by Jeanne Kelly.

Contact the publisher for information.
Printed in the United States of America.

Book design by Joe Tantillo.

Cover design by Chris Kelly.

Epigraph Books

22 East Market Street, Suite 304

Rhinebeck, New York 12572

www.epigraphPS.com

USA 845-876-4861

ISBN 978-1-9369400-8-0

Library of Congress Control Number 2011932258

Disclaimer: *All information provided in this book, The 90-Day Credit Challenge,*
is provided for information purposes only and does not constitute or substitute
for professional financial advice. Information in The 90-Day Credit Challenge
is subject to change without prior notice. Although every reasonable effort is
made to present current and accurate information, it makes no guarantees of any
kind. This book may contain information that is created and maintained by a
variety of sources both internal and external. In no event shall be responsible or
liable, directly or indirectly, for any damage or loss caused or alleged to be caused
by or in connection with the use of or reliance on any such content, goods, or
services available on or through this book or resource. This book is sold with the
understanding that neither the author nor the publisher is engaged in rendering
legal, accounting, or other professional services or advice by publishing this book.
Each individual situation is unique. Thus, if legal or financial advice or other
expert assistance is required in a specific situation, the services of a competent
professional should be sought to ensure that the situation has been evaluated
carefully and appropriately. The author and the publisher disclaim any liability,
loss, or risk resulting directly or indirectly, from the use or application of any of
the content of this book.

To my beautiful daughter, Cassandra. All of my success has been possible because you've been by my side. You continue to amaze me with your remarkable compassion for others, and I'm honored each time you call me Mom.

～

Dear Reader,

Twelve years ago, I went from being a new mom in my twenties living in a brand new house to being a divorced single mother living in a tiny cottage on my parents' farm. In picking up the pieces of my life, my first priority was to create financial independence. My goal was to get my own credit, buy my own car, and eventually buy a house.

In search of a job to make ends meet, I landed a job as a subcontractor for a credit repair company. This experience opened my eyes to what was possible. I worked hard and researched the credit industry and found out that FICO scoring is the cornerstone to financial freedom. I repaired my own credit reports, increased my FICO score, and began my new life (self-directed and in financial control). Thus, The Kelly Group was born. Since that time The Kelly Group has become one of the most legitimate and successful credit consulting companies in the United States. In 2011 I founded The Credit Owl, an online credit education service that employs the 90-day Credit Challenge you will find in this book (www.TheCreditOwl.com). Even if you can't work with me in person, the information provided in this book will help you achieve the solid credit rating you are in search of. Simply follow the steps that I took—follow the Game Plan. I hope you find the process easy to understand and are ready to begin to repair your credit today.

Warmest regards,

Jeanne Kelly

CONTENTS

I WOULD LIKE TO THANK the following people for their contributions, without which this project would have never seen the light of day.

Suzanne Kelly, who kept making sure I stayed on track to get my message across correctly. Not an easy job to work with me for all these hours. Best sister ever.

My brother, Chris Kelly, for helping me over and over again with the cover design.

Mary Kelly, thank you for being the best mom ever! You always give me your unconditional love. I love you!

Vito July 23rd, thank you for finding me. I love you. xoxo

Noel Gill, over ten years buddy, you still stick by me. I continue to say you are the best business decision I ever made.

Kelly and Cristina, through thick and thin. You work hard making sure all the clients stay on track for healthier credit.

Garry Stevens, please come back to work with me. You always help me with all my legal questions.

My editors at Epigraph, Paul and Maura, and my book designer, Joe, who helped me get this book completed at last.

.

∽

INTRODUCTION:
Playing the Game of Credit Scoring

L ike it or not, your credit score matters. Whether you're securing a home or car loan, or working to lower your mortgage or credit card rates, or even looking for a new employer, your credit score is the key to many of life's major financial decisions. But knowing how to maintain a high credit score is often less clear, and obtaining accurate information on credit scoring can be a confusing process.

I've been researching credit scoring for over ten years, and I've found that, contrary to popular wisdom, credit scores can be improved. I've developed a simple and easy step-by-step method for getting the most out of your credit score and for making sense of what may seem like madness. My method will give you more knowledge of credit scoring, give you the tools to maximize your credit score, and help you to save money on new or existing loans. And if you follow my method—the 90-Day Credit Challenge—your credit scores should improve by the end of three months.

Credit scoring is much like a game. And although learning the rules of any game will give you the tools to play, being able to play well often requires the support and guidance of a coach—someone who already knows both the possible pitfalls and the winning plays. As your coach, I want to be that support, guiding you toward stronger credit.

Eager to play the credit game?
Equally eager to win?
Let's first get to know the rules.

Days 1–30

CHAPTER
1
The Rules of the Game

This book is deliberately simple. The 90-Day Credit Challenge is meant to guide you, step by step, to do the work needed to clean up your credit reports. Although the entire book can be read quickly, some of the steps do take time, such as waiting for credit bureaus to respond to your letters or researching older payment records. But the steps are in the order they appear for a reason and each step is necessary. And depending upon your circumstances and how much time you can give, some of you may be able to work through these steps and achieve better credit at a faster pace than 90 days.

This book is slim for a reason. Goal-oriented and free of empty promises, it was written with one aim—to get you in the best credit shape as quickly as possible. Although this book is not packed with hard-to-understand credit laws or with a multitude of long, drawn-out credit success stories, in order to get in the game some basic background is necessary. So, let's get acquainted with the rules.

Rule # 1

Know Your FICO Score

Years ago, in a more personable world, creditors would sit down with loan applicants and discuss their credit history. Indiscretions, past problems, or inaccuracies were explained away with smiles and apologies. But by the 1990s, things began to change, and today these luxuries no longer exist. The handshake deals of yesterday have been replaced with a singular benchmark of approval—your FICO score.

In 1956 Bill Fair, an engineer, and Earl Isaac,

a mathematician, developed what has come to be recognized as the most acceptable model for measuring credit risk. Now known as the brain-child of the Fair Isaac Corporation, FICO has become the gold standard for credit scoring. FICO scoring is what banks and other financial institutions use to set interest rates on mortgages, home equity loans, car loans, and credit cards. FICO scoring also is used to set insurance rates, approve credit applications for revolving charge accounts (such as a department store card), assure landlords of potential tenants' ability to pay the rent, and so on. In a fairly recent trend, a low credit score may even prevent someone from receiving an offer from a possible employer, who sees it as an indication of personal instability or even as a risk of theft from the company.

Credit scores are calculated with scoring models drawn from studying how millions of people have used credit. These models assign points for different pieces of information in order to best predict future credit performance. Credit scores analyze a borrower's credit history by considering factors such as payment history, revolving balances, length of time that credit has been established, types of credit, and new credit. While the exact science of the computation is kept a proprietary secret, the FICO score attempts to condense your credit history into one single number. Whether free or with a fee, other credit reporting systems will give you a credit score, but those systems are rarely, if ever, used by lenders today. The only credit score that matters is the FICO score.

Rule # 2

Know What Your Score Means

Knowing what your score means is a necessary step in moving toward your best possible score. FICO scores range from 300 to 850. Excellent credit is 740 or above; good credit is 661 to 739; fair credit is 581 to 660; and poor is 580 or below. FICO relies on five factors to calculate a score: payment history, balances owed, length of credit history, new credit, and types of credit.

Up until about 2008, the score that most banks looked for to give out their lowest interest rates was 680. But due to the bleak financial atmosphere, that magic score has been bumped up to 740. Although several years from now that magic number may be back down at 680, it's still important to achieve the highest score possible, and not just meet the mark. As it takes time to build healthy credit, such a high score may take longer than you like, but with this Game Plan you are on your way!

The Five Factors

FICO relies on five areas of information for its credit scoring formula, which are weighted differently according to their significance as indicators of risk.

1. **Payment history** accounts for up to 35 percent of your FICO score, showing how long

you have had credit and how well you have paid on your accounts, such as mortgage loans, auto loans, credit card accounts, student loans, and business/personal loans. It also shows any history found in public records of state and county courts of tax liens, judgments, bankruptcies, foreclosures, legal suits, and wage attachments, and overdue debts referred to collection agencies.

2.   **Balances owed** account for up to 30 percent of your FICO score, and the total is based on all account balances. The ratio of unpaid balances (debt) to the total amount of credit available (credit limit) for each account is also analyzed.

3.   **Length of credit history** accounts for up to 15 percent of your FICO score and details how long your accounts have been open.

4.   **New credit** accounts for up to 10 percent of your FICO score. This is based on the number of recently opened credit accounts as well as the number of recent credit report inquiries.

5.   **Types of credit** account for up to 10 percent of your FICO score and is based on the variety of

credit you have (for example, credit cards, mortgage, auto loans, installment loans, etc.).

Rule #3

Know Your "Middle Score"

FICO scores are based on the information obtained by the three major credit consumer reporting agencies or "bureaus"—Equifax, Experian, and TransUnion. When a borrower applies for a loan, lenders obtain what's called a *tri-merge*, a combined report from all three bureaus. FICO essentially grades the information provided by each bureau. While the tri-merge is one document, it contains three separate FICO scores, one given by FICO for each bureau's information.

There are almost always discrepancies among the three reports, yielding different scores. Lenders uniformly have come to resolve discrepancies in scoring by disregarding the highest and lowest scores and relying only on the score that falls in the middle. In other words, your credit score *is* that "middle score" and *not* the average of all three scores. While lenders will receive your FICO scores with the tri-merge report, the only way for you to obtain your FICO scores is directly through FICO. The most efficient way is through the website www.myfico.com. Pay the one-time flat fee for all three scores and the reports. Ordering reports from each of the three bureaus will allow you to review your credit history, but only Equifax will allow you to purchase your FICO score. TransUnion and Experian have come up with their own scoring model, and they will try to sell it to *their* credit score, but this is not the FICO score.

In February 2009 Experian prohibited consumers from purchasing their FICO score. This means that consumers currently only have access to two FICO scores—Equifax and TransUnion. Although this prohibition is likely to change in the future, the only real way to know your accurate "middle score" today is by having a lender pull a tri-merge. Still, the two scores you receive through www.myfico.com should give you a fairly good idea of where you stand.

Rule # 4

Know Your Rights

Your credit information is protected under the Fair Credit Reporting Act (FCRA). First passed in 1970, the FCRA regulates the use, dissemination, and collection of consumer credit information. FCRA and the Fair Debt Collection Practices Act (FDCPA) form the basis of consumer credit rights and are enforced by the Federal Trade Commission. You may also request and obtain a free credit report once every twelve months from each of the three nationwide consumer credit reporting companies in accordance with the Fair and Accurate Credit Transactions Act (FACT Act).

Obtaining Your Report

Credit bureaus work independently and do not share information with each other, so you will need to obtain your credit reports from each of the three bureaus: Experian, Equifax, and TransUnion. A new service offered by all three bureaus, called 3-in-1 Credit Report, allows you to purchase a single report combining all three; however, it cannot be used to correct any errors in information because each bureau maintains its own records. It is important that you go directly to each bureau for your credit report because, in another step, you may be disputing items and you will need each individual report.

Reports can be obtained by phone, mail, or online.

Experian   www.experian.com 888-397-3742

Equifax   www.equifax.com 800-685-1111

TransUnion www.transunion.com
                  800-888-4213

You are entitled to request one free credit report each year from each of the above bureaus. A website co-sponsored by those bureaus can be accessed at https://www.annualcreditreport.com.

CHAPTER 2

Pre-Season Game

Now that you know the rules, it's time to set the groundwork for winning the game of credit scoring. In the first 30 days you will learn about your FICO score, how to obtain and read your credit reports, and how to enter into disputes directly with each credit bureau. You will also learn the value in lowering credit card balances and in securing different types of credit accounts, the impact of credit inquiries on your credit, and, perhaps most important, how much money you can save with a higher FICO score.

The steps you take in the first 30 days are crucial to increasing your FICO score. Taking these steps will enable you to make wiser credit decisions and should also make the experience of increasing your credit less painful.

Step 1

Reviewing Your Report

The first step to winning the credit game is to make sense of your credit report. Each bureau's reporting system is different. Let's go over them.

Experian

Experian is the easiest of all the reports to read. All derogatory items on the credit report are listed first, followed by all accounts in good standing.

Equifax

Equifax reports all accounts from public records, collection accounts first, then followed by all creditor accounts in alphabetical order. Because derogatory accounts are not listed in a separate section, it's important to take your time reading through each account. Any history of late payments will be listed below the creditor's name in small print.

TransUnion

TransUnion reports all derogatory items first. All accounts in good standing are listed at the end of the report.

Reviewing your reports requires great attention to detail. As you read through the reports, highlight any wrong information, including all derogatory accounts, and any accounts that are unknown to you, have a wrong balance, or report no credit limit. Also highlight any personal data that might be incorrect such as incorrect name, middle initial, address, phone number, or place of employment.

Each report also relies on a shorthand of codes and phrases. The most common are listed below.

Credit Report Codes and Phrases Key

Creditor Name = Whom the account is with (e.g., mortgage lender, retail store).

Collection Name = The collection company or agency name. In the body of the account it may also include the creditor for whom they are collecting.

Account # = The number of the account. However, the full account numbers are rarely listed on the reports, and just to really complicate things, American Express uses a different account number on the report from the one actually on the account.

Types of Accounts

I = Installment (mortgages, auto loans, personal loans, student loans, business loans)

O = Open

R = Revolving (major credit cards, store credit cards, home equity loans)

Types of Account Holders

A = Authorized user on account

C = Co-maker or Co-signer on account

I = Individual account

J = Joint account

M = Maker of account

S = Shared account

T = Terminated account

U = Undesignated account

General Account Statistics

Date opened = Date account was opened

Date of last activity = Last date account was

Date reported = Last date creditor reported account

Months reviewed = Number of months of payment history reviewed

High credit = Highest amount of loan taken out or highest ever used on credit card

Terms = Amount of months on loan

Balance = Amount due

Past due = Amount past due when report was reviewed

Payment History

30-day column = Number shows how many

times late (0 = none; 1 = 1 time over 30 days late)

60-day column = Number shows how many times late (0 = none; 1 = 1 time over 60 days late)

90-day column = Number shows how many times late (0 = none; 1 = 1 time over 90 days late)

Charge-off account = Payments have not been made in 120 days. This will soon be assigned to a collection agency.

Repossession = Auto loan/lease not paid in full and vehicle repossessed

Foreclosure = Default on property loan

Length of Reporting

Bankruptcy = In public records section for ten years. After seven years all creditors' names and account information are deleted.

Judgments = Seven years from date filed in court.

Tax liens = Seven years from paid date, but unpaid liens remain fifteen years from filing date.

Step 2

Becoming Aware of What Is Being Reported

Experian, Equifax, and TransUnion receive the information from the creditors with which you do business. They only report whatever data they are provided. For instance, you might have had a dispute with a store credit card over a purchase, and during the dispute you might not have paid the minimum payment. As a result, and unknown to you, the creditor may have reported your account as over 30 days past due. This misunderstanding could drop your score up to 100 points.

Most of us worry about obtaining credit when we need it. That's why it's useful to be aware of your credit status even in times when you don't require the use of it. Reviewing your credit at least two times a year will help to ensure that your accounts are reporting correctly.

Because hundreds of dollars paid on interest rates are potentially wasted due to a low FICO score, reviewing your report more frequently is important. Signing up to monitor your credit with www.myfico.com will alert you when something new hits your credit report. Various monitoring options are available depending on the monthly fee.

Often the smallest errors on your credit report will get in the way of securing a home loan. Two days before a client of mine was prepared to close on a refinancing of his mortgage, the lender delayed the closing. My client's FICO scores were in the 800s, so what was the problem? Upon a final pull of his credit report, the bank noticed two current addresses on his reports. Even though he had only one home address, another current address somehow found its way onto his reports. Mistake or not, minor or not, the bank would not give him the new loan without his proving to the credit bureaus that it was an error. He was able to clear up the matter, but it nonetheless delayed his closing for two weeks.

Because such a seemingly negligible issue matters to creditors, it's important to keep a regular pulse on your reports.

Step 3

What Your Credit Score Is Costing You

A divorced friend of mine, who was a single mother of three, was very excited to close on a new home. With a spotless payment history, a good income, and a sizeable down payment, her dream was nearing reality. But when the bank went to re-pull her credit report just before the closing, her middle credit score had dropped down to 675. Unfortunately, with that number, she no longer qualified for the same low interest rate. And to make matters even worse, she would have to pay an additional $7,000 at the closing table!

Credit Coach Tips

Although your FICO score is not used as the sole factor in determining whether or not you will receive a loan (other factors include the value of the home, and your employment history), your FICO score will determine the interest rate on the loan.

My friend's score had dropped because of one recent late payment on a department store credit card. Based on her good credit history, she and I were able to work with her credit card company to resolve the issue. They agreed to remove the one late payment from her credit reports, which soared her score back up to 738 and allowed her to close with the originally quoted rate.

That's why knowing what is reported on your credit reports, and possibly even knowing your FICO score, should always precede applying for a major purchase. Your score is not only important for your mortgage rate, but it can also cost you higher quotes on your car and/

or homeowners insurance, credit card interest rates, car loan/lease rates, personal loans, and more.

You can use this Loan Interest Calculator to see how your FICO score affects interest rates and payments: www.myfico.com/myfico/CreditCentral/LoanRates.asp.

But first, let's look at some examples of how the FICO score shapes mortgages, home equity loans, and auto loans.

$200,000 Mortgage, 30-year Fixed Payment

FICO score	APR	Monthly Pmt	Total Interest Paid
720–850	5.753%	$1,168.	$220,310.
700–719	5.878%	$1,183.	$226,045.
675–699	6.416%	$1,253	$251,119.
620–674	7.566%	$1,407	$306,692.
560–619	12.018%	$2,060	$541,599.
500–559	12.985%	$2,210.	$595,620.

$75,000 Home Equity Loan, 15-year Term

FICO score	APR	Monthly payment
740–850	8.083%	$720.
720–739	8.383%	$733.
700–719	8.883%	$755.
670–699	9.658%	$790.
640–669	11.158%	$ 860.
320–639	12.408%	$920.

$35,000 Auto Loan, 36-month Term

FICO score	APR	Monthly payment
720–850	6.394%	$1,071.
690–719	7.847%	$1,094.
660–689	9.844%	$1,127.
620–659	12.749%	$1,175.
590–619	17.607%	$1,258.
500–589	18.403%	$1,272.

Imagine purchasing your home for the same price as your neighbor, but after thirty years you have paid $150,000 more in interest. That's one of the many costs of a low FICO score. Your goal is to get the best rate.

Step 4

Learning the Art of Disputing

Credit reports can be quite lengthy and tedious to read through. I have come to value the use of highlighter pens! So as not to over-look anything, use them often and in a variety of colors to make disputes jump out at you from the page.

After you've carefully gone through your re-ports and made note of all problems, errors, and misinformation, it will be time to decide what needs disputing. Disputes are actions taken to rectify false reporting on your credit reports. There are two avenues for disputes. One is to work directly with the credit bureaus, and the other is to work directly with the creditors re-porting the information. It's most expeditious to first dispute directly with the bureaus. Many disputes can be resolved this way in approxi-mately 30 days.

The credit bureaus accept disputes online, but you may also work by phone or certified mail.

What I call the "nitty-gritty" of the credit game is facing late payments head on and dealing di-rectly with the creditors. But we don't want to get ahead of ourselves. That will be the work in another step. Many of the moves and plays you make will inch you toward a winning score. Those plays will also prepare you for the hard work ahead.

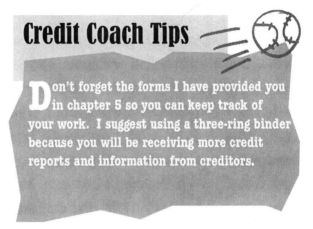

Credit Coach Tips

Don't forget the forms I have provided you in chapter 5 so you can keep track of your work. I suggest using a three-ring binder because you will be receiving more credit reports and information from creditors.

Three of the five FICO factors—account balances, new credit, and types of credit—can be worked with prior to ever entering into a dispute with either the bureaus or the creditors.

PLAY # 1: Lowering Balances

This part of your credit report includes not only the revolving balances, but all the amounts owed to all accounts (such as credit cards, mortgages, auto loans, and student loans). Because your credit report should show that you have several credit cards open with no balances or with low balances, one of the first steps to take toward raising your credit score is to review all of your accounts. If you are able to do so, make payments to lower your balances on credit cards and home equity loans as much as possible. FICO adds up all your balances and all the high credit limits, so transferring balances from one account to another will not help your score.

Paying your revolving balances down is what helps.

Balances should be paid to 20 percent of the high credit limit. This means, for example, that you shouldn't owe more than $20,000 on a $100,000 home equity loan. Being over the account limits will also lower your score. If you can't pay all accounts down, focus first on any balances over the limit, and then pay down accounts with higher interest rates.

Installment loans (such as auto, mortgages, student loans) also make up this part of the FICO score. However, score determination weighs heavier on the revolving accounts, so those are the first ones you want to pay down. Most other loans you will be keeping for the period you signed up for them. Of course they do make up part of the score. It's just not as much, so I want to focus on what is most important. This will get you the most raise in the score you possibly can within 90 days.

You want to remember that using credit is good, and if you keep the balance at 20 percent or less than the high credit limit you will get the most out of the score. You do not want to have accounts with no activity for years on the report because then they are not helping you. But they can if you just pull them out of your wallet every once in a while! For example, if you shop in a certain store and you have that store account, why not use that card and pay the bill in full when it comes in? This will keep it active and give you more points.

You want to be careful to avoid using your cards up to the limits. If you carry high balances, you are having a lot of points taken away from your FICO score. Now, you may be picking up this book at a time in your life when you have really high balances—and if that is the case, it is okay. Just start to plan on lowering those balances to help your FICO score.

FOUL!

Paying down your balances will raise your score, but closing your accounts will cause your score to plummet. At one time banks were leery of consumers who had too much available credit. But that is no longer the case. FICO scores like to see that you have credit available and that you can use it in a healthy way. Having more credit available may be just enough to give your score the boost it needs. Don't get penalized by closing accounts.

I had a client who was launching her own business. She had outstanding credit and needed to use her credit cards in order to open up her business. She didn't apply for a small business loan because she thought it might not get approved, and she really didn't need more than the credit limit she knew she had available on her credit card accounts. We met at a workshop where we were both speakers, and I went to hers. Out of respect, I think, she came to mine. At the end of the workshop she said she had learned so much about credit and that she really had no clue what her FICO score was — and now she also knew that by using her accounts she was actually lowering her score. I asked her to pull her FICO score and she was in the high 600s. She said, "Well, I know this is not horrible but I want to be in the 700s since I now own my own business." I reviewed her report and saw that she had only three credit cards and all three were being used to the limits. I gave her the suggested amounts to which they should be lowered and voilà! She focused on paying them down, and when the bureaus updated her balances her score leaped into the 700s. She said, "I just had no idea"—and again, many of us don't.

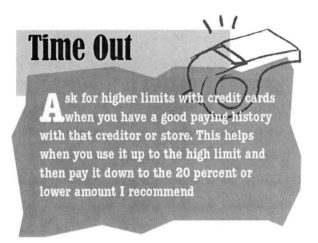

Time Out

Ask for higher limits with credit cards when you have a good paying history with that creditor or store. This helps when you use it up to the high limit and then pay it down to the 20 percent or lower amount I recommend

Play # 2: Maintaining Different Types of Credit

Because the category of "types of credit" makes up 10 percent of your FICO score, it's important to have a variety of credit on your reports. FICO wants to see that a consumer can handle a number of different accounts simultaneously. An installment loan (e.g., mortgage or personal loan), an auto loan or lease, and three or more credit cards will give you the most for this 10 percent of your score.

One client of mine called wanting to know why her score continued to drop. She said she had paid off her mortgage five years ago, paid cash for her cars, and had only been using her credit cards for annual vacations. Her score, she said, seemed to be slowly disappearing.

If you are only using credit cards and never have had a loan that you successfully paid in full, when it comes time for a large mortgage it may be difficult for you to obtain one. Even if you have the cash to pay for a substantial purchase, you may want to consider obtaining a loan with a low interest rate to build up a better history of credit. I'm not suggesting that you run out and obtain credit you do not need. But in order to maintain a healthy credit score, you need to use your credit in order to build it.

Play # 3: Disputing Accounts with Each Credit Bureau

Since credit bureaus do not share information, disputes must be conducted with each bureau based only on what they are reporting.

Each credit report includes the bureau's contact information. The fastest way to enter into a dispute is by initiating it online. It's simple to keep track by saving entered disputes to your hard drive and/or printing them for your files. If internet safety is a concern, then enter into your dispute the old-fashioned way, by snail mail. Just be sure to send it requiring certified receipt. That way there's no worry over whether or not they received your request. Calling in your disputes is also an option, but you've got nothing in writing. If you are most comfortable disputing by phone, I suggest calling five days after your initial dispute to confirm your request. Either way, the bureaus should send you confirmation of your request.

Some of the bureaus will give you a form with the report to initiate the dispute. If they do, complete the form, make a copy for your records, and mail it back to them. This can take 30 to 45 days. Otherwise, use the sample letters I have provided in chapter 5.

Common Disputes

Incorrect Personal Information

There was a time in my work when I didn't sweat the small details, like an address error or a misspelled name. But these seemingly minor details do matter to your FICO score, so it's important to make sure *everything* is accurate on your report. Check the correctness of your address, phone numbers, employment, spelling of name, date of birth, and Social Security number.

Not long ago my clients Bob and Kara came to me for help in obtaining a long overdue refinance on their home. They had excellent credit, each above 740. Their income was verified, their home was appraised, and the attorney had called to set up the closing date. But three days before the closing, the bank ran their credit one last time and their refinance came to a slamming halt.

Out of nowhere, Bob's credit reported a new address. My client never lived at that address and had nothing to do with that address, but somehow it appeared on his credit report. Unfortunately, multiple addresses are red flags for lenders, as they are a possible indication of financial responsibilities to other properties. I coached Bob to work directly with the bureau reporting the error by providing them with proof of his correct address. With my help the matter was resolved within three business days, and the closing happened the following week.

If your reports reveal a problem with your address or phone number, you will need to provide proof of your current address. Along with your dispute request, three items will be required— a copy of your driver's license or passport, a recent bank statement, and a utility bill and/or credit card bill. If your reports have the spelling of your name or your date of birth wrong, you will need to provide a copy of your birth certificate, your passport, or your driver's license. If your reports reveal the wrong Social Security number, you will need to provide them with a copy of your Social Security card, a passport, and/or a filed and signed tax return. Although these items will need to be mailed, you can initiate the dispute by phone or online.

Credit Coach Tips

During the winter holiday season and the summer months, credit bureaus are understaffed. Their vacation time will work in your favor as they have fewer staff to make verifications.

Accounts That Do Not Belong to You

If you find accounts that do not belong to you, dispute those accounts as "not mine." A creditor's misspelling of your name can create a new file, triggering more than one credit report for you. If this happens, ask that the reports be merged. Fraud and identity theft are also an issue (see chapter 4 below). Entering into the dispute with the credit bureau will tell you if the problem is a simple reporting error.

Collections, Judgments, or Tax Liens That Do Not Belong to You

If you find collections, judgments, or tax liens that do not belong to you, dispute them as "not mine" or "unaware of this debt." If you have a judgment or lien show as being released, that does not mean that it is not affecting your credit—because it is. Released does not mean removed. Released public records are still allowed to report.

Accounts Reporting Late Payments

If any accounts are reporting late payments and the information is inaccurate, initiate a dispute with that credit bureau as "never late." Or if you see an account on which you were late twice but they are reporting you as late seven times, please enter the dispute and explain that to the credit bureau. Let them do the research. Don't waste your time researching your payment history when they can do that for you. If after 30 days the late payments have not been removed and were verified, then you will need to take steps to rectify this directly with the creditors. This is usually the area where most of the work gets done.

Even if you closed the account five years ago, the creditor may stay on the report for two more years. If they are reporting positive history, leave them alone. If they are reporting derogatory information, dispute. If any of these items are verified by the credit bureaus as belonging to you, you will them need to work directly with these creditors, collection companies, or tax departments.

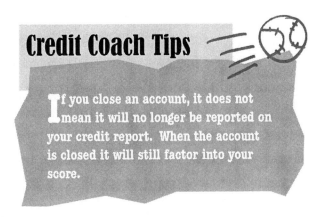

Credit Coach Tips

If you close an account, it does not mean it will no longer be reported on your credit report. When the account is closed it will still factor into your score.

·

Accounts Not Reporting the Most Recent Balance

If your accounts are not reporting the most recent balances, initiate a dispute with the credit bureau as "disputing the amount." They will contact the creditor to update the correct balance.Accounts Reporting "Joint"

A joint account is one that you and another person hold jointly. In short, this means that both parties are responsible for the account. All joint accounts will show up on your credit report (even, unfortunately, those of your ex-spouse or former partner). This does not mean, however, that your report is merged with the credit report of the other party. Because your credit report reflects your credit history alone, disputing a joint account works the same way as for an individually held account.

If you hold a joint account but no longer want your name on that account, you will need to call the lender and ask for your name to be removed. If the other party agrees to keep the account in his or her name only, the lender will, in most cases, remove your name from the account. Many times, however, the reason the account was joint to begin with was because both parties were needed for approval of the loan.

Accounts Reporting "Co-signed"

Disputing co-signed accounts works much the same as those jointly held. The account is the same as if you opened it on your own. If your co-signer makes late payments or does not pay the account at all, you are still responsible for the account. It will report derogatory on your report as well as on your co-signer's.

Accounts Not Reporting Your Credit Limit

If you have no established credit limit reported on an account, it could be affecting your credit. You want to make sure that any of your revolving accounts report a limit, as this will help your revolving ratios. You may need to contact the creditor directly to resolve this.

Step 5

Credit Inquiries

Having your credit pulled by a potential creditor is called an "inquiry," and all inquiries are listed on your credit report. Each time an inquiry is made, your credit score temporarily drops from 2 to 7 points.

When you are shopping for a big-ticket item such as a mortgage or an auto loan, if your credit is pulled for that purpose FICO gives you 30 days to rate-shop, so all of those inquiries act as one. This helps you shop around to make sure you get the best deal.

Credit Coach Tips

You have 30 days if you are shopping for a big-ticket item such as a mortgage or an auto loan, during which period all the inquiries will count as just a single inquiry.

Inquiries that lower your score are only those for which you gave authorization. If you did not allow it, then those inquiries will not affect your score. Pre-approved credit card offers that you receive in the mail, for instance, will show up on your report as "PRM" (promotional). What this means is they got your name and address, did not see anything derogatory on your report, and tagged you as a potential consumer they want to do business with. It wasn't an inquiry for which you gave specific permission.

This part of the game is fairly straightforward and simple, but it can have profound effects on your FICO score. Having come this far means that you have made a commitment to the game, and the results of your attention and hard work are on the way. With the 30 days of pre-season game cleanup out of the way, it's time for the season to begin.

FOUL!

Having your credit pulled for new credit cards, home improvement store credit cards, or just having someone pull your credit in general will hurt your credit. Before applying for any major loan, you want to have the highest score possible, so this is a reminder to not have your credit pulled four months prior to your application.

Days 31-60

CHAPTER
3
The Game

After having completed your disputes with the credit bureaus, you should have a better idea of how much work is still ahead of you. Any remaining derogatory accounts on your report mean that the creditors verified the information as correct to the credit bureaus. Because the bureaus only report the information given from each creditor, your only recourse at this point is to go directly to the creditors themselves. This part is very time-consuming, so it will take you a good 30 days. But remember, you're playing the 90-Day Credit Challenge!

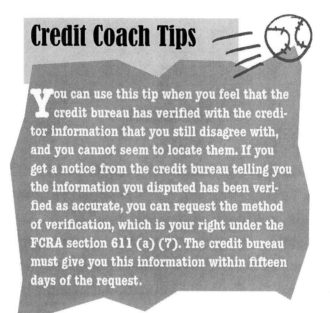

Credit Coach Tips

You can use this tip when you feel that the credit bureau has verified with the creditor information that you still disagree with, and you cannot seem to locate them. If you get a notice from the credit bureau telling you the information you disputed has been verified as accurate, you can request the method of verification, which is your right under the FCRA section 611 (a) (7). The credit bureau must give you this information within fifteen days of the request.

Step 6

Payment History

Your payment history includes the date you opened the account, your high credit limit, your balance, and how you have been paying on the account—and it follows you on your credit reports.

Begin by highlighting all the accounts that have late payments first; then I would work on the collection accounts and later the public records.

Your payment history is where you can see if you ever paid the account 30, 60, 90, or more days late. Recently a client asked me about a mortgage that seemed marked incorrectly on his report. Here is how it appeared: March reporting a 30-day overdue payment, April reporting a 30-day overdue, and May reporting a 60-day overdue. My client explained that it could not be 60 days late in May because it was paid in full in June. He did not understand that the 60-day late payment came from not paying his mortgage by the April due date, so that made April 30 days late. And since he made no payment again in May, it brought May to show 60 days late—even though he caught up his payments completely in June. So, remember this when you are reviewing the history.

Also listed in this section will be any reports of repossessions, foreclosures, settled accounts, bankruptcies, and making partial payments. These are all negative items.

In your payment history area it will also report if an account went into collection, whether or not it is paid. You may also see the term *charge-off* instead of collection. This means the creditor has sent the account to an outside agency, as they no longer were collecting on it. It hurts your FICO score the same as a collection does.

Your payment history is also made up of information in the public record section showing any judgments satisfied or still outstanding, the same as the tax liens.

The payment history is the largest percentage of what makes up your FICO score, and this is a big part of what can make your score rise or drop. You have to take the most time over this section of your report, because we want you to get the most points you can and make sure all the information on payment history is correct.

Now, some late payments are weighed heavier than others, such as mortgage late payments versus credit card late payments. Even though this is the case, each late notation is very important. For example, if you had a mortgage late payment that is eighteen months old on your report but a store credit card late payment reporting last month, the recent store credit card is going to drop your score the most. So, don't miss any of your late payments—and if you have these late payments on your report, it is time to roll up your sleeves and get working on them.

Step 7

Disputing Accounts with Creditors

Even though the fastest way to dispute derogatory reporting with the creditor is by phone, sometimes you may need to send a letter. You will know this once you've made contact with the creditor. If you have to dispute the reporting in writing, ask for the mailing address and fax number. Sample letters are provided in chapter 5.

Credit Coach Tips

For each account keep track of the creditor's name, address, phone number, person you spoke with on which date, and fax number. Use the processing form provided in chapter 5. I would add all of these forms with the detailed notes into the binder you started, because you will need to go back and forth. These detailed notes will help you in dealing with the creditors.

Once you've made the call, ask the creditor to review the late payments on your account. And be sure to tell them that the reports have been verified with the credit bureau. For example, if that creditor is reporting that you paid late (either 30, 60, or 90 days over the due date), you will want to discuss the exact reporting. What were the exact dates? Some reports provide the dates. If you have any of them, give those dates to the customer service representative. The goal of your discussion is always to try to figure out why the late payments are reporting. You want to see what they have as the exact date of getting the payment. You want them to realize that you do not agree with this reporting. You want to mention how long you have had the account and that you are a good customer, and now that you realize this account is hurting your credit you want to work to resolve it in a positive manner.

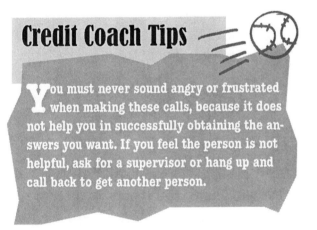

Credit Coach Tips

You must never sound angry or frustrated when making these calls, because it does not help you in successfully obtaining the answers you want. If you feel the person is not helpful, ask for a supervisor or hang up and call back to get another person.

If the late payments occurred recently, the creditor may tell you when the payment came in, and when it was due. When a derogatory report is recent, it is more crucial to your FICO score. So it is more important to get new late payment reports off. Ask the creditor to explain each late payment. If they are unable to give you this information, then ask for a written payment history so you can check their data against your records.

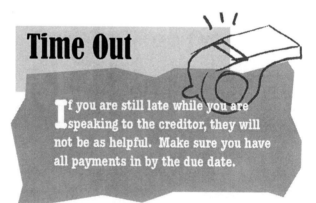

Time Out

If you are still late while you are speaking to the creditor, they will not be as helpful. Make sure you have all payments in by the due date.

At the same time, ask them to research all of the late payments. If the person you are speaking with is unable to help you, request the department responsible for research. If they know their reporting is wrong and you have proof, be sure to send it to them immediately. Proof might consist of a canceled check with a different date,

a phone confirmation code with a date difference, an envelope that was returned to you from
the post office, or evidence that they posted your
funds to another account instead of yours. Send
it with the letter of explanation. If you know they
had your wrong address, for instance, make
sure you mention it. When you are on the phone
and you know they are 100 percent incorrect, tell
them—you may not have to send in any proof. If
they still will not correct the error for you, then
you must mail or fax this proof to them with a
letter of explanation.

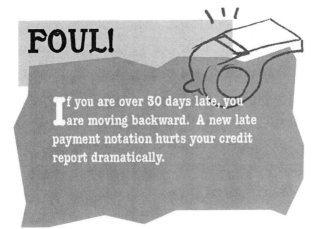

FOUL!

If you are over 30 days late, you
are moving backward. A new late
payment notation hurts your credit
report dramatically.

Step 8

Re-ageing Accounts

By re-ageing accounts, a creditor can delete your entire previous history and give you a fresh start. They still report the opening date as the same, but now you begin a brand new payment history. It all depends on the credit card company's policies. If you've been a longtime customer, they are often more willing to give you a second chance.

Many student loans will allow you to go into a program after your account is currently late or in collection with them. If you set up a payment plan making nine months of on-time payments, then they will re-age the account. You have to ask for this and be accepted into this program. Because so many people have difficulty paying their student loans in these tough economic times, it is worth the effort to take advantage of this policy to restore your credit rating.

Step 9

Requesting Payment History

A payment history will give you the exact details of when all your payments are posted and when payments were due and late fees added. This is very helpful when you need to get the exact dates of any late payments and to see the amounts due. These histories are also helpful because they sometimes allow you to see details that you might otherwise not know about. For instance, you may have sent a payment of the full balance of an account, but the next month the creditor charged a finance fee of a few dollars, causing a late payment. Since you might not have opened those statements, thinking the account was paid off, the creditor is likely to delete the late payment. Such an oversight on your part requires gentle persistence with the creditor.

Step 10

Dealing with a Collection Account

You do not want to ignore collection companies. I will show you ways to work directly with them—and if not, with the original creditor—to help resolve the account in a positive way.

Credit Coach Tips

Have a collection company stop calling you. At the end of this book there is a letter to stop the phone calls. Fax it and then send it by certified mail.

Collection accounts weigh heavily on your FICO score. And the more recent the account that has been reported, the more points that are in jeopardy. A new collection account can cost your FICO up to 100 points.

Whether it's a co-pay from a medical appointment or an outstanding phone bill, FICO does not discriminate. A collection is a collection is a collection. Regardless of the amount owed—$15 or $10,000—it means the same to your score.

Because a collection company's only goal is to retrieve the money, entering into disputes can often be a difficult process. Still, an account not belonging to you, your already having paid the bill, and/or your never receiving notification from the collection company are good reasons to dispute. But if none of these situations applies and if it is a small balance—because a settled account hurts your credit more than a collection paid in full does—the best way to resolve a collection is to offer to pay the amount in full and then request it to be deleted from your report. There is no extra fee, although if you pay over the phone you could be charged a service fee. It's more important to get the collection company off your reports.

In your conversation with the collection company they might tell you that paying on the collection is enough and that your FICO will go up even without the requested deletion. Even though down the road your score will bounce back from a paid collection, it will not bounce back immediately. In fact, after a paid collection, your FICO score will actually drop for up to six months. After six months your score will return to the number it was before it was paid and continue, with time, a slow climb.

If you need fast results for your score, it's imperative that you request the deletion.

If you need to have all open collections paid in order to obtain a loan and the collection company will not delete the information immediately, then ask the lender if you can pay the balances at the closing table with certified checks. It can give you more time to work on the account. If you have a closing in several weeks, instead of just paying the collections, you still can try to get them to accept payment for deletion. Don't pay the account in advance simply because the lender tells you they have to be paid before closing. You can ask the lender if they can be paid at the closing table and you will bring certified checks, which are as good as cash. If that's not acceptable, then you must pay the collection balances and work with them as paid collections. But this also means the rate of success for getting them deleted is much lower.

Many people think that once a collection or public record shows a debt as paid, it does not hurt their score, but it does. An unpaid balance that goes into collections and is then paid not only drops your score, but stays as a negative item on your credit report for seven years. Even though it's important to continue to work on paid collections, they are not easy to get resolved because the collection company already has what it wants—the money. But if, for example, you have five paid collections and can get two of them taken off, that helps your FICO score, so do not give up. Phone or write a letter to describe whatever dispute you might have had with the account and explain that that is why it went into collection. For instance, say that you thought this item was going to be deleted once paid, and you do not understand why it still appears. Your goal is still the same: you want this deleted/removed from your credit bureau reports. You can always add a statement of your own to your report at each credit bureau if you disagree with an item on your credit report, but this does not help your FICO score.

If you leave a collection account open and ignore it, the company will either sell it to another collection company to keep moving it around or choose to obtain a judgment. Obtaining a judgment means that the company will file suit to recover the amount owed, and the court will judge its legitimacy and then set an amount to be paid by you to the collection company or to the creditor directly.

Step 11

How to Deal With and/or Vacate Public Records

D ealing with public records, such as judgments or tax liens, requires working with the court and the reporting collection agency or creditor. When you obtain a copy of the public record, you will also have access to the contact person you will need to work with in order to get the matter resolved.

Judgments

Judgments must be worked on in the same way as open collections. The goal is to pay the account and get the reporting agency to delete it. When it comes to judgments, however, the word to use is *vacate*.

If you were never served papers for the judgment, then you should ask for it to be vacated (deleted) once you've paid it in full. If the court will not vacate the judgment, then work to obtain a settlement and pay less than the full amount owed. Similar to collection accounts, a paid judgment will drop your score for months and then your score will start to inch back up. So if you are trying to get a mortgage, wait until after the closing to pay the judgment. If the terms of your closing require that the judgment be paid, ask if you can pay it with certified funds at the closing table. If not, be sure to pay just after your credit was pulled for the final time, so the mortgage broker gets your higher FICO score. Then pay the judgment and get a copy of the satisfaction of judgment filed with the court for the loan closing.

Unlike collection accounts, settling a judgment instead of paying the amount in full may be a good option, because when it comes to judgments the credit reports show either unpaid or paid. There is no part of the judgments category where they can report it as settled or paid for a lesser amount. If they are unwilling to vacate it, then save yourself some money by asking to negotiate a settlement so you pay less than the full balance. They do not have a way to report a judgment as paid for a lesser amount than due. Ask for a lower amount to pay it off since you have to live with the judgment remaining on your credit report as paid and it will hurt your FICO score. Of course you want to approach this option more tactfully. Once you know they will not vacate the judgment when paid in full, give it some time and then call back to say you do not have all the funds but ask if there is any way they can settle on the amount that is outstanding.

Tax Liens

A tax lien works the same as a judgment. If the lien is accurate, you can do nothing but make sure it shows as released or paid (if you did pay it). Otherwise, work these like judgments—in the sense that they are public records. Get a copy of the lien that the court has on file and contact whoever listed it. If you have a dispute, go directly to the source. It may be that you were never even served with lien papers, or that there was an error in reporting and the lien was in fact released. Remember to request to have it removed completely—otherwise it will appear as if you had a lien and then paid it.

I have seen credit reports where, for years, liens reported in error were shown as released but were not deleted. Even though payment was no longer due (and if it was an error, it never had been due), the presence of the released lien on your report will negatively affect your FICO score. Getting the lien vacated will take time, with many calls and letters back and forth, but your diligence in seeing it is removed from your report will pay off in a higher score.

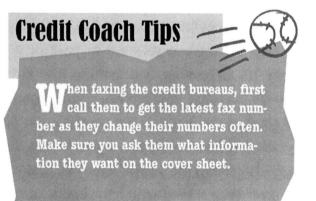

Credit Coach Tips

When faxing the credit bureaus, first call them to get the latest fax number as they change their numbers often. Make sure you ask them what information they want on the cover sheet.

Days 61-90

CHAPTER
4
Championship

Congratulations! At this point you have been working 60 days and all your hard work has brought you to the championship. Now that you've completed all the work, you should have letters in hand from either creditors or collection companies that you can send off to the credit bureaus. It is almost like disputing all over again, but now you are providing the credit bureaus with proof. It will probably take another 30 days to see this information reflected in your FICO scores. And by then you will have won the 90-Day Credit Challenge!

Step 12

Updating Data with the Credit Bureaus

Make copies of these letters of proof and mail them to the credit bureaus, directing them to delete the derogatory reporting from your account. A sample letter of this type is found in chapter 5. The deletions should occur within 30 days. If you have a pending mortgage loan closing and need the deletions right away, you can speed this up a bit by faxing the credit bureaus. Be sure to indicate at the top of your letter that it is an urgent matter that requires their immediate attention.

Settling Accounts

Once you settle a collection account, you want to make sure that you have a letter stating your account has been paid. When you settle an account, most times the letter will say "settled in full," meaning that you did not pay the full balance, but that the account has been paid.

Make sure these letters are sent to the credit bureaus immediately. Again, these updates will not help your FICO score, but leaving them unresolved will only continue to hurt it. In time your score will slowly begin to go back up. Once you've settled, be sure that your accounts then show as paid. If, in eighteen months, you need a loan, it's important that these accounts do not appear as still open or as just paid.

Credit Coach Tips

When faxing the credit bureaus, first call them to get the latest fax number as they change their numbers often. Make sure you ask them what information they want on the cover sheet.

It's almost time to celebrate. At this point a lot of work has been completed, but you want to be sure it is correctly reflected on your credit reports. You will need to make sure any letters you have received from your creditors have been updated correctly with each credit bureau. Healthier credit is in your future. But the central goals are to maintain the credit you have repaired and build new credit. As in any game, getting to the championship is great—but you want to be the big winner of a healthy high credit score!

Time Out

Wait twenty-four to forty-eight hours after faxing, and then call each credit bureau to confirm receipt. If you choose to mail the letters, send them by certified mail with a return receipt.

FOUL!

Settling accounts hurts your credit and does bring you backward in the game.

Step 13

Rebuilding New Credit

Y ou want to rebuild your credit after a major drop in your FICO score caused by a bankruptcy, foreclosure, settled accounts, late payment accounts, collections, loan modifications, or short sale (property sold for less than the full amount owed on mortgages). You may think you should do nothing with your credit at such a time but that is not the case. You need to counter the negative by building healthier, better credit.

When you have bad credit or no credit, the only place to begin to build credit is with secured credit cards. The companies who offer these financial products change deals all the time, so research the accounts to find one that works best for you. You want to try to get one that after twelve months of on-time payments will turn into a regular credit card, but even if you don't get that kind of deal it is still okay. Over time you will want to get a few new accounts. Now that you are making a fresh start with these accounts, be sure to pay everything on time. You will show that you can handle high credit limits and use your credit responsibly.

Whether you have had good credit or really bad credit, these new accounts, after some time, will help your FICO score rise.

How to Obtain New Credit

Here are four sure-fire ways to build new credit:

Open major and/or secured credit cards.

If you have no credit to speak of, not even a student loan with a good payment history, you will most likely need to obtain secured credit cards. Secured credit cards are cards you obtain by sending funds to the lender, who will then hold the funds to secure your line of credit. Although they have your money (and ordinarily the amount you send them is the same amount as your line of credit), they will not use it to make your minimum payments due. The money is held in case your account goes into collection status. It's their security.

After you've obtained the card, use it to the limit, and then pay the bill in full or at least down to 20 percent of the limit. Do this once and then continue to use your credit card up to 20 percent of your limit to keep your account active. And remember to pay on time!

Open a store credit card. Store credit cards are often more lenient with their approvals, so if you are having trouble obtaining a card from a major creditor or don't have the funds for a secured credit card, try applying for a Home

Depot, Macy's, Kay Jewelers, or Bloomingdales card. It's a good place to begin to build credit.

Credit Coach Tips

Be sure you are only working with major creditors, such as Master-Card, Visa, or large banks, as not all creditors report to the credit bureaus.

Become an authorized user on someone else's account. If you have a relative or close friend who has good credit, consider asking them to put you on their credit card account. Their entire trade line (a term for any account that is listed on your credit report from a creditor) will make their way onto your report in no time. Getting a few of these accounts on your credit report can quickly change you from having *no* FICO score to having a healthy one.

Open co-signed loan. If you have a relative or close friend who has good credit and is applying for a loan, consider asking them to put you on their pending loan as a co-signer. You would be liable for paying the loan if the signer defaulted—so make sure your friend or relative is responsible. This co-signed loan will have the same effect as being an authorized user on an account as it makes its way onto your credit report.

Step 14

Score Complications

Once you start building up your healthy credit, you will soon be able to go from paying higher interest rates to being able to rate-shop and get better deals. I want you to save money on your interest payments, and when you have a higher FICO score you will be able to take advantage of all the good deals that are out there.

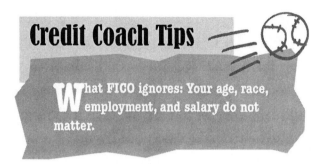

Credit Coach Tips

What FICO ignores: Your age, race, employment, and salary do not matter.

More Than One FICO Score

Sometimes, because a creditor might have entered your Social Security number incorrectly, you might end up with two files in your name. These files need to be merged together. If this happens to you, find out which credit bureau it is and call them to explain. They can normally merge the files together within twenty-four hours. You will then get a new score when your credit is re-pulled.

If you have an extra score but the Social Security number attached to it is not your own, someone else's data may have been entered in your report by error. You will also need to work with that credit bureau to explain the situation.

They will want proof of your correct Social Security number. You will need to send them copies of your Social Security card and driver's license. Correcting this normally takes a few days at most.

Although working with the credit bureaus is sometimes stressful, they do have a full customer service team who will tell you exactly how long things will take. Remember, you can always ask to speak with a supervisor.

No FICO Score

This could happen because you stopped using credit or not enough credit. You should really have a minimum of three accounts to get a good FICO score. If you have an account reporting with no activity but you never closed it, run out and use it. You can't have a score if you have no credit usage.

Step 15

How to Maintain Healthy Credit

The first step to maintaining healthy credit is to monitor your credit reports. Reviewing your credit reports twice a year will help to solve problems of false reporting, misinformation, or even worse, identity theft. It's also easier to deal with credit reporting problems when you're not in need of a loan.

Length of Credit

Although a longer credit history generally leads to a higher FICO score, applying for any new credit prior to making a major purchase, such as a new home or car, can interfere with that great history and temporarily lower your score anywhere from 5 to 30 points. So steer clear of any new credit lines within the four or five months before applying for a new mortgage or refinancing. The highest FICO score will result from no new accounts or new inquiries, low balances on credit cards, and as few as possible late payments reporting. Never close an account unless you must.

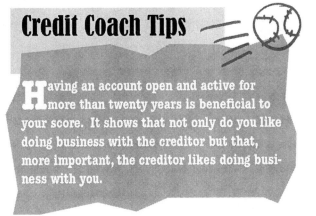

Credit Coach Tips

Having an account open and active for more than twenty years is beneficial to your score. It shows that not only do you like doing business with the creditor but that, more important, the creditor likes doing business with you.

Identity Theft

If you find only one account on your credit report that does not belong to you, it's unlikely that you've become a victim of fraud and more likely that it's an error with either the credit bureau or the collection agency. However, if you have several accounts appearing on your credit report that don't belong to you, then you may be a victim of fraud or identity theft.

If this is you, go to the police with a copy of the credit report(s) and file a police report. Before going to police you should gather some information. Contact each creditor, whether it is a creditor or a collection company, explain that these are not your accounts, and get all the information they have on you. Request them to start their own investigation. Also provide them with a copy of your identification such as your driver's license or passport, and sign your name three times below it. The investigation likes to compare a few examples of your signature, which is why I suggest you sign a few times. This jumpstarts their investigation and helps move the process along faster.

After you have spoken directly with the creditors and you have obtained a police report, call the creditors again. They should have already begun their investigation. Tell them you filed a police report and offer to send it to them. They may ask you to sign an affidavit attesting to the misinformation. However, most often they will want a letter from you stating the accounts do not belong to you. Provide them with as much as they need so they can resolve the problem as fast as possible. Urge them to send you a letter that indicates that the account does not belong to you, so that you can send that off to the credit bureau reporting the account for removal.

Credit Coach Tips

When it comes to being a victim of fraud or identity theft, you need to stay on top of the investigation. I suggest calling the creditor every three days until the matter is cleared up.

Request a "Fraud Alert" on your credit files from each bureau. A Fraud Alert will block access to your report from credit grantors until you contact them and approve their access.

Step 16

Living in an Evolving Credit World

You have now received your final credit reports back, and after this time you should have a much better report than the first one. I hope you saved all three reports from the beginning to see the difference.

Congratulations on your hard work! I hope with my help the steps went smoothly for you. Now that you have gone through all of these steps, you know exactly how to:

- Obtain your credit reports.
- Work directly with your creditors to resolve issues.
- Use only 20 percent of your revolving credit.
- Maintain healthy credit.

You've worked so hard to get here, so remember that monitoring your credit is key. But if you're as busy as I am, I recommend FICO's score watch service (www.fico.com) to help you maintain healthy credit. While you still need to be aware of my credit tips to keep building a healthy credit report, with this help from FICO you will immediately be alerted to any changes to your score.

Now that you have completed the 90-Day Credit Challenge, I highly suggest that you follow me on my website and blog, where I will continue to provide you with credit education and useful tips. Like any coach, when you reach your goal I want you to stay on top of it. Even though the game is over, life continues, and before you know it you might be in need of a new mortgage or other loan. It's vital to stay on top of your game. Maintaining what you've achieved is everything. So after you've reached your credit championship goal, keep my Five Top Rules for Maintenance in mind.

 # 1 Keep aware of what is on your credit report.

 # 2 Balances, balances, balances—keep them to 20 percent or less of your high credit limit.

#3 *Pay all the minimum payments on time.*

#4 *Inquiries—be careful whom you allow to pull your credit report.*

#5 *Maintain healthy credit—don't walk away from your credit. Pull out those cards and use them.*

CHAPTER 5

Sample Letters and Sample Forms to Track Account Disputes

Use the following letters and forms as models to write your own inquiries and requests and to keep track of your efforts. Be sure to keep copies of all documents, preferably filed in a three-ring binder.

These sample letters and forms are organized alphabetically by the title of the document.

ADD AN ACCOUNT TO A REPORT

Date:
Name:
Address:
Social Security No.:
DOB:

Report/File/Confirmation No.:
Dear Sirs:

I have the following account(s) not reporting on my credit file.

[List accounts here.]

Please contact the creditor and add the trade line onto my credit report.

After this information is added, please mail me an updated credit report.

Sincerely,

BALANCE UPDATE

Date:
Name:
Address:
Social Security No.:
DOB:

Report/File/Confirmation No.:

Dear Sirs:

The following accounts are not reporting
the correct balance.
[List accounts here]

Please update the balance(s) and send
me a new report with corrections.
(Enclosed are letters with correct
balances.)

Sincerely,

BALANCE UPDATE FORM

You might have paid several creditors. Track payments with this form.

Creditor:

Full Account No.:

Amount Paid:

Date Paid:

How was this account paid?

___ Check ___ by phone ___ Internet ___ Debit card over phone ___ Other

Creditor:

Full Account No.:

Amount Paid:

Date Paid:

How was this account paid?

___ Check ___ by phone ___ Internet ___ Debit card over phone ___ other

Creditor:

Full Account No.:

Amount Paid:

Date Paid:

How was this account paid?

___ Check ___ by phone ___ Internet ___ Debit card over phone ___ other

Creditor:

Full Account No.:

Amount Paid:

Date Paid:

How was this account paid?

___ Check ___ by phone ___ Internet ___ Debit card over phone ___ other

COLLECTION COMPANY DOES NOT HAVE DEBT

Date:
Name:
Address:
Social Security No.:

Account No.:

Dear Sirs:

I obtained a copy of my credit report and you are reporting this account.

When I called your company you explained you do not have this account **[or]** you are no longer collecting on this account.

Please send me a letter to delete this account, as you have no right to report this at this time.

Sincerely,

COLLECTION COMPANY WHO HARASSED/TO ORIGINAL CREDITOR

Date:
Name:
Address:
Social Security No.:

Account No.:

Dear Sirs:

I do owe you an outstanding balance on my account. I have had financial hardship and am trying to get my finances in order.

I am writing you at this time to let you know, though, that the company you hired or sold my account to has harassed me, and this violates the Federal Debt Collection Practices Act.

I would prefer that you recall this account and I work directly with you. Otherwise I will have no choice but to seek punitive damages against you and the collection firm.

Please contact me in writing.

Sincerely,

COLLECTION DELETION

Date:
Name:
Address:
Social Security No.:

Account No.:

Dear Sirs:

I have found your company name and address on my credit report. It is stating that I owe a balance to you.

I can pay this account in full, as long as I get this account deleted because you have never notified me.

Please let me know, as I would like to resolve this in a positive manner immediately.

Sincerely,

CREDIT DISPUTE

Date:
Name:
Address:
Social Security No.:
DOB:

Report/File/Confirmation No.:

The following information is not correct on my credit report. Please dispute the following accounts as not mine:

Account Name:
Account No.:

The following accounts are reporting late payments and I paid all on time. Please dispute these for me:

Account Name:
Account No.:

When you correct this information, please send me a new report. Thank you for your help.

Sincerely,

CREDIT LIMIT

Date:
Name:
Address:
Social Security No.:
DOB:

Report/File/Confirmation No.:

The following account(s) are not
reporting my limit:

Account Name:
Account No.:   Limit
Amount:

Please correct this information and send
me a new report. Thank you for your
time and help.

Sincerely,

DISPUTE LETTER TO CREDITOR ON FINDING INACCURATE INFORMATION

Date:
Name:
Address:
Social Security No.:
DOB:

Account No.:

Dear Sirs:

Thank you for sending me a payment history on my account. You have me listed as late during this time and this was an error.

[Insert appropriate reason for error below.]
- I moved during this time and you did not send me my bill.
- I requested an address change and you did not correct.
- I sent my check and stopped payment as you did not receive the check.
- I paid online and you did not credit on the same day.
- You misapplied my payment to my other account.

- I paid on the 30th day, not over 30 days.

- I was in the hospital and paid when I got out and was told they would waive this late report.

- I have had this account with you for a long time and was told that one time you would waive a late reporting.

Please correct this information and send me a new report. Thank you for your time and help.

Sincerely,

DISPUTE OF COLLECTION ACCOUNT

Date:
Name:
Address:
Social Security No.:

Account No.:

Dear Sirs:

I have received a copy of my credit report with your company listed on it stating I owe funds to you.

I have no idea who you are or for whom you are collecting. Please research this account as you have never notified me of this debt.

Sincerely,

DISPUTE PAYMENT HISTORY WITH CREDITOR
(first letter)

Date:
Name:
Address:
Social Security No.:
DOB:

Account No.:

Dear Sirs:

I have obtained a copy of my credit report. My account that I have with you is reporting me late. I do not agree with the reporting of:

[Insert description here]
I need you to research this information and send me a letter to correct this information.

Sincerely,

DISPUTE PAYMENT HISTORY WITH CREDITOR
(second letter)

Date:
Name:
Address:
Social Security No.:
DOB:

Account No.:

Dear Sirs:

I requested that you research and correct my account information reporting to the credit bureau. You sent me back a letter verifying the late payments. I still do not agree and I need a payment history on my account.

Sincerely,

HARASSING COLLECTION CALLS

Date:
Name:
Address:
Social Security No.:
DOB:

Account No.:

Creditor:

Dear Sirs:

Since approximately **[insert date]**, I have received several phone calls on **[insert phone number(s)]** concerning my collection account with the above-named creditor.

Accordingly, under 15 U.S.C. § 1692c, this is my formal notice to you to cease all further phone calls. Please only inform me by mail of this debt, as set forth in the federal law.

Sincerely,

IDENTITY THEFT AFFIDAVIT

Legal name:

Date of birth:

Social Security number:

Driver's License number: State:

Current address:

I have lived at this address since:

Previous addresses for past 5 years:

Phone:

Email:

Please check the following that apply:

____ I did not authorize anyone to use my name or personal information seek any funds/money/credit on loans, goods or services.

____ I did not receive any benefit, money, goods, or services as a result of the events described in this report.

____ My ID was _____lost _____stolen on or about _____

_____ I do not know who used my personal information to get any accounts in my name.

Additional information:

_____I am _____am not willing to assist in the prosecution of the person who committed this fraud.

____I am ____ am not willing to file a police report.

Attach copies:
Valid photo ID (example: passport, driver's license, state-issued ID card)
Proof of address

I DECLARE UNDER PENALTY OF PERJURY THAT THE INFORMATION I PROVIDED IN THIS AFFIDAVIT IS TRUE AND CORRECT TO THE BEST OF MY KNOWLEDGE.

X_____

_____ DATE

X_____

_____DATE

X_____

_____DATE
[Sign all three times]

Notarize:

MORE THAN ONE REPORT / FICO SCORE

Date:
Name:
Address:
Social Security No.:
DOB:

Report/File/Confirmation No.:

Dear Sirs:

You have my information duplicated so I am getting more than one FICO score, as they are reporting me as a duplicate. I am not sure if you have my Social Security number or address incorrect, so enclosed is my correct information. Please merge these reports together.

After you correct this, please send me an updated report.

Sincerely,

RE-AGE ACCOUNT

Date:
Name:
Address:
Social Security No.:
Account No.:

Dear Sirs:

I obtained a copy of my credit report and my account with you is in the adverse section.

I have called to resolve this, and now I am writing as it has been explained to me that you can re-age my account.

[If balance still on account:]
I can make a lump sum payment if you agree to delete the negative history.

I can start making minimum payments again if you put me in the program that after three months of on-time payments you will re-age the account.

[If zero balance:]

I was told you can re-age the account and remove the negative information from my report. I would like to do this and start fresh on this account.

Thank you for your help in resolving this in a positive manner.

Sincerely,

RECORD OF COLLECTION PHONE CALLS

*Creditor*_____
*Phones*_____

Date & Time	Comment

Account #_____
History_____

REMOVE MY NAME FROM ACCOUNT

Date:
Name:
Address:
Social Security No.:
DOB:

Account No.:

Dear Sirs:

This account is appearing on my credit report (enclosed is a copy), but this account does not belong to me. Please send me a letter to remove this account from my credit report.

Thank you for your help in resolving this issue.

Sincerely,

CPSIA information can be obtained at www.ICGtesting.com
Printed in the USA
266574BV00001B/1/P

9 781936 940080